Enjoy The Ride:
What My Bike Taught Me
About Managing People

Enjoy The Ride:
What My Bike Taught Me About Managing People

Courtney K. Berg SPHR

ISBN 10: 0986367605
ISBN 13: 9780986367601
Names and certain details of the stories mentioned in this book have been changed to protect the privacy of the people involved. However, we have attempted to convey the essence of the experience and the underlying principles as accurately as possible.

Editors: In Contact, Inc., Nancy C. Berg

Designer: Jason Sornsuwan

It is strongly recommended before you change any policies or practices in your business you obtain the advice of legal counsel to ensure compliance with the law.

I dedicate this book to my dad, who taught me so much about life and business. Although he no longer is on Earth, his memory and his spirit are always in my heart.

Table Of Contents

Introduction

I have always loved to ride my bike. As a kid, it gave me freedom to get places faster, to be more independent, and it was fun. I enjoyed biking so much I had day-dreams of being a professional stunt biker.

One day, I rode my bike to the park to practice some tricks. I went to the top of the hill and sized up the decline. On this day, I wanted to have a new and different challenge, so I decided to lie down on the seat as I rode. With my stomach on the seat and my feet off the back, I started my adventure down the hill. I was a little unsteady at first and had to shift my center of gravity to avoid disaster. Once I regained my balance, I realized I hadn't thought this trick all the way through. As I came roaring down toward the bottom of the hill, I saw the truck. It was blue and coming fast - way too fast and I had to think quickly. I remember hearing the screeching of brakes as I sped by the front grill of the truck, racing to the far side of the street where I slammed into the curb. My front tire jolted to an abrupt stop as I flew over the handlebars and landed squarely on my back in the park grass.

The truck sped on. There was no one else around and I was on my own. At first I wasn't sure if I could move. I looked up to see what appeared to be puzzle-pieces of dark green tree leaves surrounded by baby blue sky. I was alive. That was a good start though I realized everything hurt. I was relieved to be able to roll over without anything feeling broken. My leg had a cut, most likely from hitting the rock that was nearby. I had some sore spots that would turn into deep bruises but otherwise I was ok.

My thoughts turned to my bike. I raised my head to see what damage had been done. I stood up slowly, to ensure I wouldn't fall back down again and staggered toward my mangled bike. The front tire rim looked like a kidney bean. After seeing the damage I knew that I was going to have to tell my Dad about the wreck. Asking for help was difficult for me: I was my father's daughter and learned to be self-sufficient from the best. But I was a kid and if I didn't ask for help, I wouldn't have a bike to ride. Somehow I managed to drag my broken self and my bike, along with my battered pride, back to my house. When I walked into the house, my Dad was amidst his weekend morning routine of reading the paper and drinking coffee. "Dad? I have a problem."

Dad looked up and saw my scraped-up body and the well of tears in my eyes. He put down his paper, "Are you OK?"

I nodded. He listened calmly as I recounted what had happened. I told him that I realized I had made a bad choice and that I wouldn't do it again. "I am so sorry Dad. I will use my allowance to pay for the repairs but I need help to get my bike to the repair shop."

Dad got up, walked over, and put his arm around me and said, "We can always fix a bike. I'm just glad that *you* are ok!"

My Dad always created a safe environment in which I was able to learn from both my successes and mistakes. When I succeeded at something, we celebrated. When I made a mistake, we discussed what I could have done differently and then worked together on correcting it. I felt comfortable talking to my Dad about my bent bike rim and wreck, as I knew he would support and love me unconditionally. I *knew* that if I told him the truth, we would work together on the solution.

Not everyone has this kind of upbringing. Many people experience fear when they make a mistake and are reluctant to admit an error. What we experience as kids impacts how

In order to establish an atmosphere of success, managers must provide an environment in which employees feel comfortable in not only making mistakes, but also with discussing them in an open way.

we deal with life and work issues as an adult. This is especially true with mistakes, conflict, and conflict-resolution. Employees are no exception and are, not surprisingly, reluctant to come forward with their shortcomings. Nothing illustrates this concept better than how employees conduct themselves in the workplace, particularly under stress. I have seen employees who have gone to great lengths to hide mistakes they have made. Employees often fear that admitting to mistakes makes them appear unqualified or incapable of doing their job. The old adage, *"if you are not failing once in a while, then you are not taking enough risks"* really is true. Both employee successes and failures should be freely discussed and even *encouraged* so that real innovation and growth are possible.

Experiences with both bicycling and with my Dad have been the hub of my management wheel. The lessons I learned have shaped how I work with people. My father was an incredible manager - a quintessential people-person - and had a strong influence on the professional I am today. In the following pages I share my experiences bicycling and managing, and how life-lessons learned from both are not so dissimilar. My hope is that, through these stories and guidelines, you will find management to be as easy as riding a bike; difficult to learn and balance, but once you get rolling there is nothing quite like the feeling of the wind on your face while riding down a smooth path. Enjoy the ride.

CHAPTER 1

The Right Equipment ▪ Hiring Employees

Many years ago my family and I were at Dad's house celebrating his 70th birthday. The gifts had just been opened and we were picking up the wrapping paper strewn on the floor. Dad was laughing, telling a story about teaching me to ride my bike. Suddenly, we heard the unmistakable "click, click, click" of a bicycle being rolled down the hall. Wearing a new bike helmet and bike gloves, my stepmom Beverly entered with one last present - a beautiful new silver and black mountain bike. It was perfect for Dad. It was the perfect color, the perfect size and the perfect gift.

As much as they loved bicycling it was short-lived. Just two years later, my father passed away and Bev surprised me on my birthday with his bike. I was honored to be the steward of something he loved so much. Along with his bike she gave me all of his gear. Wearing his gloves and helmet gave me a sense that Dad was with me as I rode the trails close to my home. I replayed the conversations in my head that we'd had and wisdom he infused into my life. It gave me peace.

Over time, I reluctantly realized the bike was too big for me and was impacting my ability to ride efficiently and safely. His helmet was too large and his gloves were impeding the agility of my fingers on the handlebars and brakes. I loved my Dad and wanted him with me on my rides, but I realized he would be very disappointed if I jeopardized my safety by using the wrong equipment. He would always tell me I needed the right gear to ensure a safe and successful ride. Dad's philosophy of having "all the right tools" was prevalent in all aspects of his life. Whether at work or play, he always surrounded himself with the proper equipment and right people he needed to get the job done.

As a great manager, Dad had a way of gaining his employees' respect and trust. He took his time when hiring staff to ensure he brought-on the people who could handle customer needs. He had a specific interview process and put great effort into finding the best person for the job. Although he had remarkable intuition when it came to reading people, he was still very methodical in his approach. He did not want to hire the wrong person and regret it down the road. He also knew that just because someone had been an outstanding sales person for another company, they might not be the right fit for *his* company.

I was reminded of this one day as I rode his bike. What was the perfect bicycle for Dad turned out not to be the perfect bicycle for me. Just as the right bike is key for a successful biking experience, selecting and retaining the right people is paramount to your business success. Your employees are an extension of you. Your customers will interact with your employees on a regular basis. Still, when many business owners determine they need to hire someone, they tend to think in terms of right now and not in terms of the future. They have an opening they need to fill, so they hire the first person that meets their most obvious requirements. This short sightedness leads to multiple problems down the road.

A few years ago, Tom, an overwhelmed business owner asked me to help him select a new employee. He had run an ad and received several resumes, narrowed his search to his top two contenders, and wanted an outside opinion before making an offer.

After listening to his pro and con list for the candidates, I asked him, "Why are you hiring a sales person?"

He said, "I have too much to do and I need help with sales."

"What are you doing each day?" I asked.

"Oh, I'm answering the phone, sending quotes, handling order processing and complaints, and doing the invoicing; all while trying to get business in the door. I just need someone to do that part."

"Who can sell your products better than you?" I asked.

Tom paused for a minute and said, "I'll teach them how to sell my products."

"Ok, but can they sell your products, the products *you* developed and are passionate about, as well as *you* can?" I asked.

"No," Tom admitted.

I followed with, "But what about all of the other work on your plate? Wouldn't it make more sense to get someone to invoice, answer the phone and process the orders? Say, an administrative assistant who could free up your time so you could go out and sell more?" He looked at me with such relief and said, "That makes so much sense. Thank you!"

Before you even think about hiring someone, you need to know your organizations' goals and needs. What do you want to accomplish in the next three to five years? For example: do you want to increase revenue, the number of units sold, the number of employees hired, or develop a new product? Whatever your goals, ensure they are **SMART** goals: Are they **S**pecific? How do you **M**easure success for these goals? Are they **A**ctionable? Are they **R**easonable (can you attain them)? Are they **T**ime-oriented?

Next, decide what positions are necessary to achieve these goals. For each position determine:

- What functions are necessary
- Roles and responsibilities
- General expectations
- Knowledge, skills, and abilities (KSA's)

    ○ **K**nowledge is what they know

- ○ **S**kills are the things they can do
- ○ **A**bilities are those characteristics that make up their personality and generally cannot be taught.

- ▪ Determine if the KSA's are required or preferred and at what level (basic, intermediate or advanced). For example, if Microsoft Office is required, what level of proficiency is required at the time of hire and what knowledge and skills can be taught to the employee?

Your next step is to write a job description or summary that accurately defines the position. Write your expectations, the minimum and preferred qualifications, the working environment and the stress factors, the mental requirements, and the equipment used in that job. See Appendix B for more information on job descriptions.

Only once you are clear about what the position requires, do you then sit down to write and place an advertisement that outlines the roles, responsibilities, and expectations of the job along with the KSA's necessary. Consider the best medium to use when placing an ad: online, social media, newspapers, magazines, trade publications, and/or emails. You do not need to include everything in the advertisement, but you should be sure to include the essential functions of the job and the minimum requirements. In addition, include how they should apply (email, fax, phone), to whom they should apply, and other items you would like them to include such as a cover letter, salary require-ments, or a list of references.

Once you have the candidates' resumes and the other credentials requested, conduct an initial screening process. To do this effectively, first determine the basic criteria that will be used to sort through the initial group of candidates. Screening criteria could include: the ap-plication instructions were followed, the minimum qualifications are met, and work history lends itself to the job advertised. Determine strong candidates for the position by reviewing the applications. Reject any candidates who do not meet the criteria.

The second step in the screening process, which usually occurs via phone or email, is to ask the remaining candidates 4 to 6 ques-tions. These screening questions should determine if they meet your minimum qualifications for the position such as: licenses/certifications, minimum experience levels, ability to travel, proven sales experience, and the like. It is prudent to document each step of the screening process to establish how the candidates were elim-inated from consideration or moved on to the next step.

Now it is time to design the face-to-face interview questions that will guide the interview to determine if the selected candidate demonstrates the KSA's to meet the expectations of the job. The best interview questions are behavior-based that ask for specific examples of past performance and give insight into the candidate's educational background and work experience. Consider if there is testing that needs to be done as part of the process, such as computer skills.

It is now time to schedule face-to-face interviews. The interviews should be approximately 45 to 60 minutes in length and the candidates should do the majority of the talking. Take objective notes outlining their answers. Ensure your interview questions are work related and do not violate employment laws. See Appendix A for more information on interviewing.

Behavior-Based Questions

Asking a candidate this type of question helps to understand how the candidate acted in the past and is a good indicator of how they will most likely act in the future. Lead your questions with the phrases, "Give

Behavior-based questions are the key component to finding the right person for the job.

me a specific example of," "Tell me a time when," and "Describe a situation that." It is not necessary for the job applicant to give examples that apply directly to your specific business. What *is* important is their thought process and decision making ability? For instance, if a candidate describes an issue with team members while on a group project, it doesn't matter what the issue is about, so much as how the candidate handled the teamwork issue. Did he/she run to the supervisor to say that the team was falling apart? Did he just complete the project himself without dealing with the team or the issue? Or, did she do nothing and use the issue as an excuse for missing the deadline or for the poor quality of the final project? A perfect applicant might say he worked with the teams' differences, found common ground, and finished a quality project on time despite team issues. A skilled interviewer needs to listen for clues that can predict a prospective employee's behavior.

Remember to review the job description, the expectations, and the KSAs they need for successful performance of that particular job. Take this information and develop additional behavior-based questions that draw out what they have done in the past and predict whether or not they have the necessary skills for the job. Keep in mind, skills are trainable - attitudes and behaviors are not. Make a mental note of anything that is a deal-breaker for the job. Keep in mind that someone who was great somewhere else *may* not be the best person for *this* job. I often see this when people move from corporate work to small businesses or when they hire someone very *likable*. They like them so much they just <u>know</u> they will fit in at this job. If they don't meet all of the requirements for the job, then you are setting them up to fail. See Appendix C for some sample interview questions.

Extending an Offer

Once the face-to-face interviewing process is complete and you have selected your top 2-3 applicants, it's time to contact their references. This will help you narrow the field and determine the best candidate for your position. Once your selection is clear, a verbal offer can be made. This verbal offer is contingent upon the completion of new hire paperwork, background check, motor vehicle check, and drug screening. You can send the offer packet to the candidate as long as you set a clear deadline for the paperwork to be completed and returned. I recommend you complete background checks no matter the size of your business. A third party should complete all background checks. Once the candidate completes the paperwork and successfully clears the background check, you can extend a final offer. Should a candidate not pass one of the background check criteria, you must notify them and follow The Fair Credit Reporting Act notification legislation. For full details, visit the Bureau of Consumer Protection Business Center on the web.

www.business.ftc.gov/documents/

bus08-using-consumer-reports-what-employers-need-know

Only after the chosen candidate has cleared all the hiring requirements and accepts the final offer do you then reject candidates not selected and place other top candidates on a waiting list. To place a candidate on your waiting list, explain that you were impressed with their credentials and that they interviewed well, however, another candidate was selected for this position. Explain that you would like to keep them on your waiting list and will contact them should another position become available that matches their background and skills. Invite them to contact you every month to check in. Keep these resumes handy for approximately one year. On occasion, candidates back out of job offers, take another offer, or simply do poorly in their first few months – so it is good have these resumes on hand.

There are other final administrative tasks you must complete once you hire an employee, which include:

- Submit an E-Verify on their I-9 information to ensure they can legally work in the United States
- File employee documents with the State New Hire program
- Conduct orientation to inform and prepare your new employee for onboarding

Offer and Reject Letters

Providing offer letters to your candidates is a best practice. A formal written letter can be extended once the vetting process is successfully completed and a verbal offer has been made. The formal offer letter should include an outline of the job, job title, the wage and frequency, reporting structure, and start date. Be careful not to make the offer

All too often, an offer must be rescinded due to an issue in the background check. letter look like a contract. Most states are "at will," meaning that either you or the employee can end the employment relationship at anytime for any reason without notice. An employment contract may negate that right. To protect the at-will relationship, state the "employment is at will and can end at anytime for any reason." This cannot be stressed enough; give the offer letter to the candidate only *after* they have passed all background tests and other screenings. Again, make sure you have kept a few backup candidates to call if your first choice doesn't work out at the job.

Rejection letters are also a best practice. Not only does it let the candidate know that their application process is closed with your organization, but it also is a good public relations tactic for your business. Candidates will thank you for letting them know that the process is complete. Remember, candidates, their friends and families are also prospective customers. They will share that you treated them fairly and that is good for your business.

Federal Employment Laws That Impact Hiring

The size of the company dictates the employment laws you must follow. Regardless of size, there are several laws all employers must adhere to. Some of these laws may not apply to you, but it is important to be familiar with them. If you have questions, seek the advice of your attorney or a Human Resource professional. Following is a list of important laws to keep in mind:

TITLE VII OF THE CIVIL RIGHTS ACT

EXECUTIVE ORDERS 11246, 11375, 11478, AND 12138

CIVIL RIGHTS ACT OF 1991

AGE DISCRIMINATION IN EMPLOYMENT ACT

REHABILITATION ACT

AMERICANS WITH DISABILITIES ACT

PREGNANCY DISCRIMINATION ACT

VIETNAM ERA VETERANS READJUSTMENT ASSISTANCE ACT

IMMIGRATION REFORM AND CONTROL ACT

UNIFORM GUIDELINES ON EMPLOYEE SELECTION PROCEDURES

WORKER ADJUSTMENT AND RETRAINING NOTIFICATION ACT

CONGRESSIONAL ACCOUNTABILITY ACT

PRIVACY ACT OF 1974

EMPLOYEE POLYGRAPH PROTECTION ACT (1988)

CONSUMER CREDIT PROTECTION ACT (1968)

FAIR CREDIT REPORTING ACT (1970)

GENETIC INFORMATION NON-DISCRIMINATION ACT (2008)

As your company grows, the list of laws you must comply with also grows. It is wise to have a labor attorney and HR consultant that you can consult with when you have questions regarding any of these required laws.

CHAPTER 2

Learning To Ride ▪ On-Boarding
Your New Employee

My Dad was a remarkable man. He was my role model, my hero, and my friend. Dad taught me about life and instilled solid values that I live by every day. As he taught me to ride my bicycle, he was clearly weaving life lessons into our time together. "Get back up, try again," "Everyone falls down before they succeed," and "You have to persist if you want to reach your goals!"

I remember what seemed like a never-ending summer, he and I would go outside and I would try to get up the courage to ride on my own. But, I was afraid. It seemed that if I went too fast, I would fall off. If I went too slowly, I couldn't keep the bike upright. It was a constant struggle and balancing act. If I thought that Dad was hanging onto the bike, then I would be fine. But the thought of him letting go created such a fear response in me that he had to talk me down.

"What if I fall?" I worried.

"What if I hit something?"

"What if I look stupid?" Fear definitely brought out the worst in me.

On the day of my first solo ride, Dad ran behind me and held on to my bike seat. I knew that if I fell, he would be there to catch me. It gave me confidence. As a kid I didn't think how impossible it would have been for him to *actually* keep me from falling or hitting the pavement. And then it happened. As I started riding and was gaining some speed, I looked for Dad and he was running beside me - and definitely not holding on! "*What ifs*" started popping into my head and I instantly started to falter.

But, Dad started cheering me on, "You can do it! You are doing great!"

My confidence returned with his soothing voice, the bike became steadier, and I then realized that I could go faster on my own than I ever had before. Dad was so proud of me when I rode down the street all by myself. But the coolest thing was that so was I. His positive reinforcement allowed me to get over the bump of self-doubt and allowed me to soar.

Hiring a new employee is similar to your child's first bicycle lesson. Kids need help in understanding how to finely balance this new way of moving and playing with a bicycle. If Dad had just handed me the bike and said, "Have fun, let me know if you need anything," then it would have taken me months to learn how to ride. After falling so many times and getting banged up and hurt, I probably would have decided I didn't really like riding my bike and would have just found something else fun to do. Learning to ride a bike can be hard and outside of our comfort zone – it's new and has a lot to do with balance and self-confidence. The key to learning how to ride a bike lays in understanding the distinction between moving fast enough so that you don't fall off of it and moving slow enough that you do not lose control. The time-held saying, "*it's like riding a bike*" rings true because the skills, balance, and focus to stay upright are never *unlearned*.

New employees find themselves in a similar situation. They have left the comfort of their previous employer's environment and brought with them the general principles and skills needed to work

Employers with great on-board-ing practices and structure will accomplish these goals and create an atmosphere of success.

within their position. They will need more information about your organization in order to be successful in their new environment. They need to learn the systems, processes, daily duties, and responsibilities so they can find their balance in your company. Solid on-boarding processes include two parts, company orientation and job training.

Orientation teaches them the specifics within your unique landscape. The new employee is then assigned to work with a mentor for training. Typically, the mentor is someone in the new-hire's same area of expertise who can not only work on day-to-day activities with the employee, but also provide resources and troubleshooting that he or she will need in order to be successful.

There are many ways of designing new employee on-boarding processes. Some businesses have a checklist that is completed as the employee moves from task to task. Some businesses have a more formalized orientation with managers teaching various important aspects of the business. Others just grab whoever is walking by the orientation room and ask them to come in and talk about what they do. The way orientation is handled within an organization depends upon the organization's environment and available resources.

There are several topics that need to be covered in orientation. New employees need to understand the big picture regarding company history, company expectations, the mission and vision, and how their job fits into the organizational goals. In addition to this, other topics should be discussed such as: company policies and processes, security, time clock, computer login, phone etiquette, and how to handle customer complaints. Giving your new employee a tour of the office and introducing them to their co-workers is a must.

The second part of the on-boarding process that acquaints new employees to the organization is job-specific training. This type of training is designed for the new employee's distinct job or area. The mentor or trainer is the one who will work with them to ensure they know how to accomplish daily work and responsibilities such as: using computer software, general work activities, how work is assigned, how to prioritize, how to handle customer issues, the best resources for issues that arise, and other topics that will enable the employee to succeed on a day-to-day basis.

As their employer you are holding onto the back of their bike as they gain balance in their new environment. Once you know they are up to speed and can manage on their own, step back and let them ride. Giving encouragement, "You're doing great!" or "I know you can do this!" is an amazing confidence booster for new hires. If the on-boarding process is done well, the new hire will make good decisions without always having to consult with you. "Letting go of the bike seat" is nerve-wracking for both employer and new employee, but is really the only way to let them work freely and with confidence.

CHAPTER 3

On-Going Tune-Ups ▪ Conducting Check-Ins

The local bike shop where I bought my bike had magnificent follow up process. Within a week, I received a card from the shop to come back in and get 10% off biking shorts. Two weeks later, I received a note from the manager thanking me for my purchase along with a bicycling magazine that had great articles that were specifically about the type of bicycle I purchased – a cross bike. Two weeks after that, I received an email from the manager asking how I liked my bike and telling me about various classes held at their shop. What great customer service processes these folks have! Not only were these contacts excellent sales tactics, they made me feel comfortable going into the shop and talking to their technicians. I was invited by the manager to

The conversation an employer has with their employee starts on day one of the hire and continues throughout their tenure.

visit with the staff and find accessories that would work for me. The manager was building rapport with me so that I would come back to *her* shop when I had a concern or a need. Whenever I return to the shop, the manager greets me and the technicians help me find whatever I am looking for or make suggestions for something that would make my ride more enjoyable. And as all shop managers know, having a customer browse in a shop is great for sales. I picked-up many items I thought might be helpful or fun on my rides.

Managers are quick to nurture relationships with customers to ensure they return to the store and, hopefully, make a purchase again. They want to be the *go-to* for customers in their industry. Unfortunately, many managers don't take the time to nurture their *employees* in the same manner that they have their customers. It is important to meet with your new employee often to make sure they have what they need to do their job and to understand what is expected of them. This process is called a *check-in*.

A check-in is an on-going interaction between a supervisor, manager or business owner and an employee. They are designed to build rapport, determine if there is anything the employee needs to better accomplish his or her goals and aspirations, and establish a line of dialog that develops trust and respect between the employee and his or her supervisors. Each check-in paves the way for easier conversations down the road. Just as the relationship I had with my Dad was nurtured over time, it made difficult conversations easier - like when I wrecked my bike. This type of relationship is essential for clear and open communication with employees. They should feel secure enough to share good and bad news.

Typically, the way to start a good check-in conversation is to ask questions. Be inquisitive about their work or how they are doing with the new clients, protocols, or procedures. Some questions you could ask include:

- What went smoothly in your week? What didn't?
- Do you need anything to help you do your job better?
- Are you finding everything you need; i.e., office supplies, training materials, and helpful colleagues?
- Are your questions being answered?
- How do you feel your training is going?
- Have you met other staff members and have a sense of what they do?
- Have you found someone to eat lunch with?
- Have you had a chance to review the employee handbook? Do you have any questions?
- What has been the biggest challenge you've faced since you joined our team?

Check-ins should be more frequent at the beginning of an employee's career with your business and taper-off over time, however they never stop. There may be times that the number of check-ins increase based on the employee's performance. Check-ins create an atmosphere of success with employees – it makes them feel that you are genuinely interested in their success and want to give them the training, tools and support they need to do their job. Additionally, they won't be afraid to come to you for help. Continue to develop and nurture your relationship with your employees, and in return, you will not only secure loyalty and independence, but also increased productivity.

CHAPTER 4

Keeping Track of Your Distance ▪
Performance Evaluations

Cycling technology has grown significantly so I decided to visit local bike shops to look for the best cycling computer to keep track of my speed and distance. I discovered that I could download an app to my smartphone that keeps all my information in one place. This app tracks total miles, total time, and multiple speed statistics including: current speed, fastest speed, average speed, and it even calculates the calories burned on the ride. It also has a map feature which makes it easy to see the distance traveled and how far is left to go – not to mention, I never get lost! The stats for each ride can be saved so I can compare rides and ride further and faster the next time.

Just as I want to know about the progress I am making on my bike, employees want to know how they are progressing as well. They want to know if they are meeting expectations, the things they have done right, and what areas they need to focus on. Human resources professionals identify performance evaluations as a formal way to measure an employee's progress and as a helpful management tool. In the last several years, there has been controversy surrounding the use of performance evaluations or appraisals. It has even been trendy to shun the performance review for employees, especially in smaller businesses. There are many books that outline the pros and cons of these reviews. More often than not, I hear performance evaluation opponents say that performance should be evaluated on an on-going basis and not just once a year. I agree. However, a company does not need to choose between having performance evaluations once or twice a year and providing constant and timely feedback to its employees. These are not mutually exclusive. Both techniques should be used when it comes to employees. That said, what is the best way to handle the evaluation of employee performance?

Just as the bike app motivated me to go a little farther than before or maybe a little bit faster, managers should think of themselves as an *employee app* that gives feedback, not on a computer, but via the check-in. The manager should have an on-going conversation with each employee. In the previous chapter, I introduced the concept of the check-in, which establishes the foundation of the relationship between the manager and the employee and offers a way to have short yet meaningful conversations with an employee about a multitude of topics. Beyond orientation and on boarding, topics can include how the employee feels about the job, customers, software, equipment, and the training. This conversation can also be used to fine tune the employee's work product and help the employee learn alternative ways of handling situations in a non-threatening manner. It develops a rapport that is helpful in trouble-shooting work scenarios and eases an employee's mind about interactions with their supervisor. The relationship developed through check-ins is the springboard for subsequent conversations. Employees will feel more comfortable discussing issues, problems and even mistakes because the foundation has been created. Just as a bicycle app motivates me to improve my efforts, an effective manager motivates an employee to demonstrate what they are capable of achieving or improving.

When evaluating how well an employee has done during the evaluation period, a manager must consider the employee's performance on the job based on the outlined expectations. The foundation for these behavior and job performance expectations must be laid throughout the entire employment process. The employee should have a solid understanding of his/her job description, the manager's expectations, and the knowledge, skills, and abilities that are required for the position. The only way to ensure that occurs is through communication between the manager and the employee. The communication of the expectations should happen continuously from the time of the interview, through the orientation and training, all the way to the time when the employee separates from the company. It must be constant and ongoing. Nothing in a performance evaluation should be a surprise to the employee unless something happened within 24 hours of the evaluation meeting.

Often I hear managers say they would rather go to the dentist than meet with an employee to evaluate their performance. Their concerns include: the performance evaluation process takes too much time, they don't want to share negative information, the form doesn't evaluate what the employee does in a meaningful way, no one takes the processes seriously – it is just another item on their to-do list. Just as a good checkup with the dentist is a good practice for your health, evaluations can be a chance for you and your employees to address issues head-on and improve the health of employee performance. See Appendix D for a sample performance evaluation.

Designing a form and process that is meaningful to both employer and employee and one that evaluates the proper information are key components to an effective performance evaluation.

Sometimes it takes just a few steps to turn a meaningless evaluation process into a successful one. The majority of the work behind a successful evaluation process is in the preparation of the meeting. Below are seven key steps to ensure you are getting the most out of your formal review process:

1. Set an appointment with the employee and give them a self-evaluation form to be completed and returned prior to the meeting.

2. Review the employee's job description, KSA's, and any other documents that were given to the employee that pertains to the areas in which they will be evaluated.

3. Review prior notes and evaluations in the employee's personnel file to see if there are any on-going issues, accomplishments, or positive or negative feedback from others.

4. Compare the outlined expectations for the employee and what they have accomplished during the performance period.

5. Did the employee improve on the areas of weakness in the performance period?

6. Gather feedback from other employees, managers, or clients who have worked closely with the employee.

7. Based on all the information you collect, begin completing the performance evaluation document.

The process involved in reviewing an employee's performance can appear tedious. However, it is time well spent. The review is an invaluable tool that can either justify a pay raise or help defend in a wrongful termination suit. It can also ensure objectivity and fairness. The performance review process enables you to provide

Employees are the most important and most expensive resource for the company.
formal documentation of the employee's performance in conjunction with any issue that arises during their tenure. Just as a bicycle computer tracks and records my bike ride information, the performance review tracks and records an employee's performance. With that information, it is easier to adjust the employee's course to ensure success.

Management Evaluation Questions

As part of an evaluation process, it is beneficial to ask questions about the effectiveness of the management team. These questions are used to understand how your management style resonates with your employees. In many cases, your employees will be apprehensive about sharing this information directly with you. You may want to consider having an outside resource facilitate the discussion or conduct a survey for you.

Following is a list of possible questions you can use to determine how the supervisor is doing according to an employee:

GENERAL QUESTIONS

Do you trust your supervisor?

Do you like working here?

What can your supervisor do to help you be more motivated or productive?

MOTIVATION

Does your supervisor recognize your job performance or accomplishments? How often?

What obstacles are in the way of doing your job? Please explain.

Do you feel your supervisor is overly critical of your performance? If yes, why?

QUALITY OF RESULTS

Does your supervisor complete tasks, follow up and accomplish goals?

Do you feel that your supervisor holds other members of the team accountable for accomplishing their goals? Please explain.

PROBLEM SOLVING / DECISION MAKING

Does your supervisor appropriately consult employees when making decisions affecting the department?

Does your supervisor give you the appropriate level of decision-making for your position? Why or Why not?

DELEGATING DIVERSITY

Does your supervisor delegate assignments to others?

Does your supervisor distribute tasks and projects fairly and to the appropriate people? If not, please explain.

Does your supervisor delegate too much, too little, just the right amount?

It is important to use this information once you receive the employee's feedback. If you gather this information and do nothing with it, you will most likely damage your credibility with the employees. If they ask for changes that cannot be made, explain the reason the changes cannot be made. Employees want feedback and find great value in your candor in those situations.

CHAPTER 5

Yelling Isn't the Answer • The
Progressive Discipline Process

M y Dad wasn't a *yeller*; of which I mean of the shouting sort. I can only remember a handful of times that he raised his voice and the one and only time he spanked me. Despite the lack of raised hands or voices, I knew what he expected of me. He expected me to be polite and respectful to others,

Dad clearly saw the difference between who I was and how I behaved.

learn from my mistakes, logically consider my options, and to determine the best course of action.

My Dad communicated expectations every day without being intimidating or threatening. Regardless of what I did, I was never fearful he would stop loving me. This is why he was such a good parent and manager. The ability to separate a person's essence from their behavior is a key component of being a good manager.

My Dad saw the goodness in people and trusted that they could improve upon their behavior. And when they didn't, he had a conversation with them about their actions, stated his expectations, and told them he was there to help but their ultimate success depended on them.

His counseling didn't always work; sometimes he had to fire people. It was never a surprise to the employee. The employees he fired knew it was going to happen because they had been warned, counseled and coached prior to the termination meeting. He wanted them to succeed. Try as he might, an employee may be in the wrong position, the wrong business, or simply not have the ability or motivation to change their behavior. This difficult situation can cause constant grinding - like a gear that won't change or a chain that rubs with every crank; everything moving slow, rough, or coming to a halt.

Long before a termination takes place, there is an awareness that a problem exists and action must be taken. To be in alignment with business best practices, management needs to initiate the discipline process. The goal of any discipline process is to turn the employee's behavior around. We all want to hire and train exceptional people. We spend a great deal of time planning to hire, interviewing candidates, and making sure they have all the tools and support to do the job. When the tools and support aren't enough, disciplinary action is necessary to ensure the employee understands the consequences of not meeting the established expectations and goals.

Before engaging in discipline, it is important to try to understand the root cause of the problem. Refer to your Employee Handbook to review office policies and procedures as well as the laws and regulations that apply to your profession. Is the root cause of the problem a behavior, training, or knowledge issue? Is there a barrier preventing the employee from doing what you want them to do? Or, are there outside forces that are impeding the employee from performing?

I like to describe many of the managers I work with as using *progressive frustration* in lieu of *progressive discipline* when it comes to correcting employee behavior. When these managers first see unwanted behavior and choose not to speak to the employee at that time, they are practicing progressive frustration. Inevitably the manager becomes more and more frustrated over time, all the while procrastinating about talking to the employee until something snaps and the final straw is placed upon the proverbial camel's back. At this point, the situation is unmanageable and the frustration is so great that hastily firing the employee becomes the only option. Rather than taking time to discuss the behavior with the employee upfront, the manager hits their boiling point and loses control. Progressive frustration has never, in my experience, yielded positive results.

Progressive discipline is a much better approach. It is progressive in the sense that with each undesired or repeated behavior, the discipline process becomes more formal. When a behavior is identified that is not meeting expectations, the manager should privately talk to the employee about the situation. Sometimes the first conversation, called awareness counseling, is all that is necessary to change the employee's behavior. Seeing an employee walk into the office late and pulling them aside to say, "Hey, I noticed you were late this morning, is everything ok?" can do wonders. The conversation is not confrontational - it is inquisitive. To the employee having the manager ask if everything is ok is one of concern. Being pulled aside by the manager who asks one simple, seemingly harmless question also allows the employee to know the manager is aware he or she came in late. That one insight may prevent the employee from being late again. If that were the case, the discipline cycle would be complete. More typically, however, and management must get a little more formal and the next time the employee is late, pull them aside and give them a verbal warning, "I visited with you last week when you came in 20 minutes late and asked if everything was ok. You assured me it was. Today you came in 30 minutes late. Your coworkers rely on you to finish your customer report by 9:00 a.m. so they can start contacting clients and ensuring we are addressing their needs. When you come in late, it postpones our ability to contact those customers and could lead to bigger problems down the line and a tarnished company reputation. You need to be here at 8:00 a.m. in order for our office to function at its top level of efficiency. This is a verbal warning. I know you can turn this around and I am here to help you, but if this continues, we will be having a more serious discussion."

Letting the employee know that you remember addressing this issue before and that they are moving down the progressive discipline path is important. They need to know this is a verbal warning and the next step will be documented in their employee file. Make note of the conversation and place the note in the employee's file for future reference.

Written warnings are the step in the discipline process most owners and managers dread the most. They feel boxed in. If they don't give the written warn-

Hope as managers might, very few employees recognize the significance of their actions and correct it on their own.

ing, then it is likely the employee will continue on with their unacceptable conduct. Giving a written warning causes anxiety, conflict, and it is uncomfortable. It is so easy to postpone this step until there is less turmoil or to wait for just the right time. This is understandable, but a major mistake. Given the anticipated outcomes, managers don't see a high likelihood of changing their employee's actions, so they put up with the poor behavior and hit a frustration point where termination is their only answer. The written warning is an important document and if skipped, the company is left vulnerable to a costly wrongful termination lawsuit.

Preparation for issuing a written warning is imperative and should include: your expectations, the fact that the employee is not meeting those expectations, dates of past meetings and conversations, what actions you expect from the employee and a timeframe to show improvement. When meeting with the employee, discuss all of these elements with them before giving them the written warning. A conversation between you and the employee will be more productive than reading the warning. The written warning is an important document, along with the conversation, to reinforce the importance of the situation and should be given to the employee after you have discussed the issues with them. Once discussed, have them review the document and ask if they have questions.

There may be more than one written warning given to the employee depending upon the situation and a second written warning may be warranted if a similar situation occurs. A copy of the warning should be placed in the employee's drop file and the original signed warning should be placed in the employee's HR file.

How you discipline your employees directly impacts your liability in regard to unemployment insurance, discrimination claims, and wrongful termination suits. A solid discipline process enables all managers to handle employee issues consistently and fairly. It is helpful to remember that it is the employee's *behavior* and not the employee themselves that has brought you to this point. They have the power to correct this issue, and when they choose not to, discipline and/or termination is the result of that choice. The following overview of the discipline process will help guide you through the 7 steps to coaching and disciplining an employee.

THE 7 STEPS OF PROGRESSIVE DISCIPLINE

1. **Identify** the employee's behavior that is not meeting expectations.
2. **Review** the potential cause(s) of the problem, for example: training, knowledge, barriers to success, and outside influences.
3. **Talk** to the employee and make them aware of your concern about their behavior. This should be done in a non-threatening way. The employee should feel you support them and that you believe they can correct the behavior. This step is called **Awareness Counseling**. You should make note of the conversation and place the note in the employee's file for future reference.
4. A **Verbal Warning** is given if the behavior continues after Awareness Counseling. In this step of the process, you tell the

employee they are not meeting your expectations. Remind them you had a previous conversation and tell them how you expect their conduct to change. If their behavior doesn't change, you will be moving down the path of written discipline. Assure them you have confidence they can fix the problem and you are here to help them, but their ultimate success is up to them.

5. A **Written Warning** is necessary if the employee does not correct their behavior after the Verbal Warning.

6. When there are continued problems or issues, a **Final Written Warning** is imperative. This is the employee's last chance to correct their behavior before suspension or termination occurs.

7. **Termination** is the end result of the discipline process. Ultimately, the employee is at a crossroads of deciding to either change or to seek employment elsewhere. Terminations are difficult, yet are made easier by using the progressive discipline process because the problem has been addressed in a consistent and reasonable manner. Some positions, companies, or restrictions are just not a good fit for some employees. This can be a chance for the employee to find something that better matches their goals, and a chance for the company to find a more capable and productive employee.

CHAPTER 6

Letting Go Of the Bike ▪ Employee Termination

F iring an employee should never be taken lightly. It's important to remember that every employee is someone's father, mother, son, or daughter with obligations, dreams, and lives to live. Ideally, both the employee and your company are working to achieve mutually supportive goals. When that is not the case,

"If they are causing disruption, then they just need you to help them take that final step."

and the employee isn't happy, productive or involved, it becomes necessary to part ways. In some cases, this gives the person a chance to reevaluate what they want to do and pursue something that they like or are good at doing. When I got my first assistant manager job at a local movie theater, when I was seventeen, I was having trouble with an employee, who was also my friend, and decided to ask Dad's advice on what to do. Dad's advice helped me terminate my friend in a professional way. Dad reminded me of the time he taught me to ride a bike. He said, "You wanted me to hang on to the back of your bike seat forever, but I had to let go so that you could experience riding on your own. Although I worried, I let go."

Sometimes, employees are not able to ride on their own, are riding haphazardly or in the wrong direction. In HR we often say we don't fire employees, they fire themselves. We just do the paperwork. It's true. Employees may want to take their bike in a different direction than the organization is headed. If that is the case and the employee does not respond to coaching and discipline, they must be fired. The best outcome from this process is that both the management and the employee have gained something from the experience. Managers must realize that some employees are just not salvageable and, just like my kidney bean-shaped bike tire, need to be replaced.

Very few terminations are black and white. Managers know it is time to terminate an employee because they have consistently worked with the employee with little or no improvement. Yet, they still question if today is the right day. I firmly believe in the management mantra of *slow to hire, quick to fire*. If we take time to hire employees and do it the right way, there will be fewer terminations. It would be rare to buy a bicycle that is just right for you without asking a lot of questions, trying it out, and reviewing all of the features. You would probably have spent hours online browsing brands and gadgets.

And so it is with the process of hiring; the more groundwork you lay in preparation for the new hire to match their knowledge, skills, and abilities to the position, the less likely that termination will be necessary. Trouble begins when a dynamic and eager person is hired that lacks the KSA's required for the position.

When it becomes clear that further action must be taken and you have gone through all of the steps of progressive discipline and decided that termination is the next step, do it quickly. Again, it is a common mistake to delay the termination or give the employee one more chance. Remember, what you do for one employee you must do for all employees or risk litigation of favoritism, sexism, or other discrimination.

Prior to termination, it is important to review the employee's file to ensure the decision is indeed correct. I recommend an attorney or human resources professional review the file for any potential issues that could come up after the termination regarding discrimination, not following an established procedure, and the like. Once satisfied with the decision to terminate the employee, this simple planning process can help with this difficult management task:

1. Prepare for the meeting with the employee by summarizing the reasons for termination and practicing what will be said in the meeting. It is perfectly acceptable to refer to notes during the meeting.

2. Find a private location, an office with the door shut, and schedule the meeting when there will be no interruptions. It is best to handle a meeting of this nature when clients are not in the office.

3. I recommend having a witness present, usually an office manager or human resources professional, to take notes and observe what occurs during the meeting. Avoid having other employees present as this might embarrass the employee.

4. The meeting format should include:

   a. The reason for termination. Remind the employee that there had been several meetings addressing their deficient behavior and that company expectations had been clearly defined. Even though the expectations were known, the employee was not able to correct their behavior. As a result, employment is being terminated. The meeting should be short and non-argumentative. If the employee wants to argue, explain that ample time to correct the behavior had been given. Emphasize the decision has been made and although their feelings are understandable, this is not a discussion.

   b. Give them their final paycheck as required by state law. You can contact the local Department of Labor for regulations about the timing, what is owed, or other legal obligations regarding a final check in your state.

c. Ask the employee to go to their desk and gather their personal belongings and directly leave the building. Go with them as they do this. This is an uncomfortable, but necessary step for the safety of other employees, the terminated employee, and you. If employee's attitude or anger appears to be a problem, prepare by having people available to help control the situation.

5. Do not tell the rest of the employees their co-worker was terminated or engage with others as the employee is leaving. Later, simply state their co-worker no longer works with your organization. They will have many questions and may be concerned that they too could be terminated. Stress to the staff that these types of decisions are not random and assure them that they are necessary to the success of the team. It is equally important to stress there will be no further discussion as it would be in violation of privacy laws. Assure them that employee meetings are not discussed with others and that if they have concerns or questions about their performance they should talk to management.

6. Write a memo to be put in the employee's files outlining the reasons for termination, the notes from the termination

meeting, and any incidents that occurred as the employee was exiting the premises. These notes could be subpoenaed and need to be factual and not subjective.

7. Process any paperwork necessary regarding the terminated employee's benefits: COBRA/health insurance, and retirement.

Safety

No two employees react the same way to the news of their termination. Regardless of prior coaching or number of verbal or written warnings, their reaction can be a surprise. Even employees, who had been with the company for a number of years and had been outstanding but now do not meet expectations, can turn on a dime when they are terminated. Workplace safety should be a significant concern to both business owners and employees. There is far too much in the media about disgruntled employees behaving badly. Consider this true story.

It started with a call from a panicked business owner, "She won't give me back the company cell phone and she's deleting stuff off the company computer!"

"Who?" I asked, concerned that the voice on the other end was very anxious.

"Jackie," he said.

I asked what happened.

He told me he had finally had it and decided to fire his long-term employee. She had been with him from the beginning, but recently her performance and attitude had taken a turn for the worse. She was absent more than present and often late when she did arrive. Her work quality had degraded to the extent that much of her work had to be checked and redone. Recently, she was more argumentative and disengaged from her co-workers and clients. Jackie used to have a go-getter attitude, but now seemed to struggle to get even minimal tasks done. It wasn't surprising that she had pushed the owner to the point of termination, but worse, her actions now were all defiant and obviously devious.

"What should I do? I can't get her to leave her office, she won't give me the cell phone and she is doing who knows what to our computer system!" His voice was raised and he was obviously panicked about what she could be doing to his client data and proprietary software. His mind was full of what he was going to have to do to recover from her vindictive actions.

I had to be very specific in my direction to him. "You need to hang up with me and go into her office with your cell phone in hand. Tell her that unless she puts everything down and walks out of the building right now, you *will* call the police. Make sure you are willing to follow through on your threat because she may not stop or give you your phone. Can you do this?"

This business owner, a physically strong man, was concerned for the safety and integrity of his business and wanted to protect it. This was not business as usual. He said, "I'm willing to do whatever it takes to get her out of my office."

The owner called me later that evening and told me that he did end up calling the police. They had to physically remove her from the office. In their investigation that day they uncovered that the employee was dealing drugs out of the office using her company issued cell phone and laptop. Had the owner not called the police, the employee could have deleted important company data. As you might imagine, it could have caused big problems for the company and its clientele. Luckily, she was just trying to cover up her illegal activities and had no intention of sabotaging his business.

Most terminations do not involve drug dealers, employees refusing to give back company owned property, or the police. However, terminations are an emotional time for both the employee and the employer and anything can happen. Be prepared by having a strong termination process and procedures in place to follow that ensures everyone's safety. Be especially aware if your employees carry any sharp tools that are potential threats of harm or any actual weapons as with law enforcement. Awareness of potential harm or injury is half the battle in assessing safety and potential risks in a termination procedure.

CHAPTER 7

Enjoy Your Ride

On a beautiful Sunday morning, I woke up and saw the glorious blue Colorado summer sky. The temperature was perfect for a long bike ride. I was dressed and on my bike almost immediately. I have ridden bikes for so long that they now seem to be a part of me; I go from cement to gravel to sand and I instinctively adjust my balance as riding surfaces change. I am able to stop concentrating on the mechanics of riding and truly enjoy the landscape and environment around me.

On this ride, I stopped along the trail when I spotted a Crane cooling off in the creek. I enjoyed the sounds of the birds and the coolness of a light breeze on my face. It was a wonderful day for a ride. Later on in the ride, I hit a rough spot in the gravel and my tire started to slide. My instincts kicked in and I immediately recovered. For a moment I remembered the fear I had when I first started riding. It took many miles of practice and experience to learn the skills and gain the confidence to manage that fear and stay upright on my bike. Dad always encouraged me as we rode, side-by-side, up and down our block. He and I both knew I was ready to ride alone and learn how to manage the challenges that all cyclists encounter. Now I love to ride and feel confident that I can handle any terrain and keep my balance. It finally makes sense to me what Dad was saying, "Now that you have mastered the tough part, you can sit back and really enjoy the ride."

Managing employees is similar to bicycle riding in many ways. Just as Dad provided a safe environment, the right equipment, and ongoing guidance to learn how to ride a bicycle, employees need your and help and support to gain their balance in finding their own style in a new work environment. A good manager will not stop there, but will ride side-by-side to coach the employee through each challenge to find the best solution. There will come a time when the employee has gained the confidence to apply what they've learned to independently navigate the rough terrain. Finally, an excellent manager maintains regular communication, encouragement, feedback and guidance; always leaving the door open to celebrate successes and learn from mistakes. Owners and

It is the responsibility of the employer to hold on to the back of the bike until the employee is stable and ready to do their job.

supervisors, who properly manage their team with the confidence and certainty that comes with experience, create an atmosphere of success. That is my hope for all of you. *Enjoy the ride!*

APPENDIX A: Do's and Don'ts of Interviewing

The characteristics of a good interviewer include the ability to:

- Make the applicant feel comfortable
- Make an objective decision
- Understand and look past an applicant's fears and anxieties about interviewing
- Make the hiring recommendation in a timely manner

A good interviewer can interpret an applicant's behavior, expressions and body language in an objective manner. The interviewer can engage in personal conversations without becoming emotionally involved in the subjective matter.

It is important to refrain from criticizing or interrupting the applicant as they answer questions. Interruptions will put the applicant in an uncomfortable position and tends to create poor interview responses. Allow them the opportunity to express themselves during the interview. If you feel the responses are taking too long, let them finish their current answer, and explain that there are many questions and limited time to get through them. Ask them if they would be comfortable moving through the questions a little quicker and if you need clarification you'll ask them a follow up question.

How to conduct a group interview:

Inform the candidate in advance it will be a group interview. If you can, let the applicant know who will be in attendance along with their titles so the applicant can properly prepare.

- Set up the interview room so the applicant can easily see all the interviewers. Make sure there is enough space for the size of group expected.
- Coordinate who will ask each question so the applicant doesn't feel like you are not prepared to meet with them.
- Ask one question at a time. If you have a follow up question out of turn, ask if you might ask a follow up question.
- Do not have side conversations with the group in front of the candidate.
- Do not respond to the applicant's answers.

Documenting the Interview:

- Do include objective comments about the interview and the candidate's answers
- Do not include physical appearance, handicap, or any subjective comments
- Do not document things about their physical characteristics such as young, old, good-looking, blond, gray hair, athletic, and the like
- Do not document personality types like stupid, overbearing, nerdish, weak, or other similar descriptors

Points to remember:

- Anything you write can be used in a court of law
- Comments should be related to the job and contain evidence to support the decision to hire or not hire the candidate
- All comments should be related to how the candidate does or does not meet the job qualifications
- Comments regarding whether or not the candidate was professionally dressed are acceptable

- If the candidate is not a good fit, document why with specific reasons, for example "The candidate was rude to our interview panel and was used profane language."

Do NOT ask questions regarding:

- Age
- Sex
- Race/National origin
- Number or age of children
- Church/Religious preference
- Marital status/Sexual orientation
- Arrest record
- Spouse's occupation
- Candidate's or spouse's pregnancy, or intent to have children
- Disability or any other health problems

DO ask questions that:

- Are part of the structured interview process
- Help you learn about their past work experience
- Relate to bona fide occupational qualifications (BFOQ's)

Make sure the candidate has had adequate time to:

- Expand on his/her qualifications
- Answer the questions completely
- Provide evidence of his/her proficiency and knowledge

At the end of the interview, you should ask yourself:

- Does the candidate have the qualifications for the job such as, education, certification, and experience?
- Are the candidate's values and work style compatible with your company culture and work environment?

APPENDIX B: Sample Job Description

State or federal law does not require Job descriptions. If there were such a thing as a natural work law, I would argue job descriptions would be required. Following is a sample job description for your reference.

Position Title:

Reports To:

Number of Direct Reports:

Status: Non-Exempt   Exempt   Full-Time   Part-Time

Date:

Summary of Expectations: In this area briefly describe what is required from the person in this position including responsibilities and results expected, for example:

The Office Manager will be responsible for the overall operation of the office management for ABC Dog Biscuit Company. It is a position that requires excellent customer service, organizational and time management skills; a knowledge of bookkeeping, computer software packages, and general human resources practices. It is expected that the Office Manager has advanced written and verbal communication skills, advanced professional and interpersonal skills and is strong at balancing multiple tasks at one time.

Required Duties and Responsibilities:

The Required Duties and Responsibilities section lists in bullet format the duties and responsibilities of the job. It also lists expectations including confidentiality, time management, and client interactions. Here are some examples:

- *Responsible for overall office administration*
- *Complete duties of a confidential nature, client contracts and correspondence as well as HR matters*
- *Advanced knowledge of computer/software packages; including Word, Excel, Power Point, Studio IT and Outlook*
- *Provide consistent and timely follow up to all clients and associates regarding projects, questions and issues*
- *Responsible for bookkeeping including: client invoicing, proposals, purchase orders, accounts receivable and payable, ordering and tracking product, bank reconciliation and sales tax*
- *All tasks associated with daily mail*

- *Create and maintain employee records for employee related issues such as absences, time off requests, reviews and revision of payroll*
- *Ability to facilitate staff meetings*
- *Special projects and duties as assigned*

Minimum Qualifications:

This area describes the job related qualifications that are necessary to be considered for the position also presented in bullet format. It typically includes knowledge, skills and abilities that are required for the incumbent to be successful in the position. Examples include the following:

- *Full-Time Employee*
- *High School diploma or equivalent preferred*
- *Ability to read, write and speak the English language fluently*
- *Ability to communicate with clients and co-workers in a friendly, positive, respectful manner*
- *Ability to maintain a professional demeanor, even under pressure*
- *Strong listening, oral and written communication skills*
- *Demonstrates a goal oriented attitude through words and actions*

- *Effectively utilizes available resources to achieve goals*
- *Ability to efficiently handle multiple tasks at one time*
- *Ability to work evenings, weekends*

Stress Factors:

This section describes the stress factors associated with the position and, to the extent possible, the frequency in which those factors will be confronted. Examples include:

Occasionally: Collections, angry clients

Frequently: Intensive tasks, long hours

Working Environment:

This section describes the working environment and conditions. It also describes the frequency in which those environmental factors will be experienced. Examples include:

Occasionally: Works alone, works during scheduled time off, extended days, temperature changes, wet and/or humid conditions, noise, vibration, mechanical equipment, electrical equipment, travel

Frequently: Works around others, verbal contact with others, works in office environment on a computer, works with office equipment

Mental Requirements:

This section describes the mental requirements necessary for success in the position. It also describes the frequency in which those mental abilities will be encountered. Examples include:

Occasionally: Memorization, higher math skills, writing proposals

Frequently: Simple and complex reading and writing, statistics, critical problem solving, significant attention to detail, critical thinking, development of action plans and problem solving, perception, computation and simple math skills.

Constantly: Judgment, reasoning and decision-making, interpersonal interactions

Equipment used:

This section describes the equipment used in the position. It also describes the frequency in which those equipment items will be used. Examples include:

Occasionally: Paper cutter and 3-hole punch

Frequently: Computer, printer, keyboard, computer files, calculator, paperclips, pens/pencils, file folders, filing cabinets, paper, pager, cell phone, notebooks, scissors, manual stapler, telephone, copy machine, fax machine

DISCLAIMER: *This position description is not designed nor intended to cover or contain a comprehensive listing of activities, duties or responsibilities that are required of the employee. Other duties may/will be assigned dependent upon business need.*

_____   _____

Employee Signature   Date

APPENDIX C: Sample Interview Questions

GENERAL BACKGROUND:

1. Resumes help outline someone's work experience and education, but I think it really comes to life when someone talks about those experiences. Could you bring your resume to life for us?

2. We all have had positive and negative experiences in our past positions. Please describe these for me and tell me why these experiences stand out in your mind.

3. What job has been the most frustrating for you? Why was it frustrating?

CUSTOMER SERVICE:

1. Tell me about a time you were faced with being unable to meet the customer's needs.

2. Describe a time when you faced the situation where you had to stand up to your boss in order to meet a customer's needs.

3. We all say things we wish we could take back. Tell me about a time you said something to a customer you wish you hadn't. How did you repair the damage that conversation caused?

DECISION MAKING:

1. Describe a time you faced having to shoot from the hip on a decision because you didn't have all the information you needed.

2. What is the worst decision you've made at a job? Why does this incident stand out in your mind? What did you try to do to rectify the situation?

3. We've all had to communicate a supervisor's/company's decision that we don't necessarily agree with. Tell me about a time you've had to do that.

COMMUNICATION:

1. Tell me about a time when you could not get your point across to someone.
2. Describe a time when an employee came to you complaining about a policy.
3. Describe a time when you withheld important information from a boss.

TIME MANAGEMENT:

1. Describe a time when you had to manage multiple priorities at once.
2. How do you know what tasks you need to accomplish?
3. Give me an example of a time when a burning issue changed your priorities and interrupted your day. What did you do? What did you do with the items that were on your to-do list that had to be bumped?

TEAMWORK:

1. Describe a time when a team you were on did not meet the deadline.

2. What can you share with me that will prove you are a team player?

3. Describe a team environment that did not work. What made it not work? What would you do differently to improve the situation?

SALES AND MARKETING:

1. Why do some people succeed at sales and some people fail?

2. Finding new clients is imperative for the success of small business. Describe how you find prospects for your current company.

3. Selling can be difficult at times. What has been your greatest obstacle in selling? How have you overcome that obstacle?

SYSTEMS AND PROCESSES:

1. Describe a time when you developed, or helped develop, a new system or process. Why did you feel the system needed to be developed?

2. Give me an example of a system that you have altered or disregarded to get the job done. Did you communicate your work-around to anyone? Why or why not?

3. Do you feel employees should be consulted on every systems/process change within an organization before it is implemented?

STRESS MANAGEMENT:

1. How do you deal with the day-to-day stress of your work environment?
2. What in your current job is a stress inducer?
3. We all can feel overwhelmed from time to time. Tell me about a time that has happened to you. What did you do to mitigate your stress level?

RESULTS ORIENTED:

1. What is the most important aspect of an employee's performance: the process of getting results or the results themselves? Why?
2. Do you consider yourself to be detail oriented? Give an example of a time when you had to be detail oriented. What was the hardest part of that assignment for you?
3. Give me an example of a time when you did not get the results for which you were responsible. What happened and what did you do?

PROBLEM SOLVING:

1. Do you have a system or process you use when making decisions?

2. What is the most unique way you have dealt with a problem you have encountered at work?

3. What is the most difficult customer problem you have had to resolve? How did you resolve it? What was the result?

VISION AND PURPOSE:

1. Do you feel the vision and mission statements are an important part of an organization?

2. When have you seen a manager disregard the organization's mission? Did you confront the manager? Did you go to his/her supervisor?

3. How does a company mission/vision impact the way you interact with co-workers, supervisors, or clients?

APPENDIX D: EMPLOYEE PERFORMANCE EVALUATION

The following categories are used when evaluating an employee's work performance. Based on the position the employee is responsible for, some categories may or may not be appropriate. The employee is rated based on which best describes their performance over the entire review period.

Meets Expectations: The employee is doing a satisfactory job. Their performance in every area is competent and constructive. They are qualified for their position. They meet all minimal job expectations.

Exceeds Expectations: The employee's job performance is noticeably better than that of their peers. There are only one or two areas in which they are not entirely proficient. They routinely exceed expectations. The quality of their performance and their results are an example for others. You consider them a great asset to the organization.

Superior Performance: The employee's performance has been genuinely outstanding. Other employees talk about this employee's high quality of work. The quality of their work is so outstanding that no rating other than "superior performance" could even be considered. No one would dispute that they are one of the most talented individuals in the organization.

Met Required Knowledge, Skills and Abilities (KSA's): YES **NO** (Circle correct answer. Make notes regarding specific KSA's that were not met and develop action plans to ensure they will be met in the future.)

Met job description roles and responsibilities: YES   NO (Circle correct answer. Make notes regarding specific roles/responsibilities that were not met and develop action plans to ensure they will be met in the future.)

Work Quality: The employee demonstrates a commitment to quality through their everyday actions.

_____Below Expected   _____Expected _____ Exceeds Expected _____Superior

Productivity: The employee is organized in processing work and an acceptable amount of work is accomplished on a regular basis.

_____Below Expected   _____Expected _____ Exceeds Expected _____Superior

Teamwork: The employee willingly helps and works with others through building and maintaining relationships with others.

_____Below Expected _____Expected _____ Exceeds Expected _____Superior

Technical Competence: The employee has proven the skills and acquired the licenses/certifications (if applicable) necessary to effectively perform the job.

_____Below Expected _____Expected _____ Exceeds Expected _____Superior

Overall Job Efficiency: The employee does accurate, thorough, neat and timely work as well as offering suggestions to help the office run more efficiently. S/he works well with minimal supervision.

_____Below Expected _____Expected _____ Exceeds Expected _____Superior

Sales Techniques: The employee quickly establishes rapport with prospect or client through listening to prospects' needs and properly matching the company services. S/he does not have unqualified prospects in counted in pipeline reports.

_____Below Expected _____Expected _____ Exceeds Expected _____Superior

Business Development: The employee continually searches for new clients and demonstrates the ability to gain customer commitments to new business.

_____Below Expected   _____Expected   _____ Exceeds Expected
_____Superior

Networking: The employee maintains contacts and builds relationships over time. S/he attends appropriate networking events as assigned by management and effectively communicates the company's mission statement bringing more interest to the company.

_____Below Expected   _____Expected   _____ Exceeds Expected
_____Superior

Problem Solving Skills: The employee demonstrates a strong ability to identify, analyze, and solve problems. S/he handles problems quickly and effectively. S/he routinely comes to you with a problem and solution options and/or their recommendation for a solution.

_____Below Expected   _____Expected   _____ Exceeds Expected
_____Superior

Customer Service: The employee demonstrates the ability to anticipate and find solutions for customer's needs. S/he recognizes the root of the problem and seeks help from the appropriate people when necessary.

_____Below Expected   _____Expected   _____ Exceeds Expected
_____Superior

Attitude: The employee consistently demonstrates positive interactions with others, their job, and the organization.

_____Below Expected   _____Expected   _____ Exceeds Expected
_____Superior

Initiative: The employee demonstrates ability to begin and follow through with a plan and takes action without prompting or direct supervision.

_____Below Expected   _____Expected _____ Exceeds Expected _____Superior

Dependability: The employee carries out assigned tasks to completion. S/he does not miss deadlines for assignments and falls within the company's attendance guidelines.

_____Below Expected   _____Expected _____ Exceeds Expected _____Superior

Communication: The employee exhibits effective communication skills with management, employees, and customers in a welcoming and non-confrontational manner. S/he utilizes discretion with confidential information.

_____Below Expected   _____Expected _____ Exceeds Expected _____Superior

Embraces Growth and Change: The employee accepts change within the organization with professionalism. S/he makes asks questions about changes in a non-confrontational manner.

_____Below Expected   _____Expected _____ Exceeds Expected _____Superior

Self-Motivator: The employee accomplishes assignments and daily work and moves on to the next project with minimal supervision needed.

_____Below Expected   _____Expected   _____ Exceeds Expected

_____Superior

Employee Signature: _____ **Date:** _____

Employee Printed Name: _____

Manager Signature: _____ **Date:** _____

Manager Printed Name: _____

APPENDIX E: Progressive Discipline Steps

AWARENESS COUNSELING:

Awareness counseling is like a gentle reminder. For example, when an employee comes in late to the office, a supervisor can say "Good morning, Bob, I noticed you came in late this morning. Is everything ok?" This lets the employee know that you noticed he came in late. Many times, that acknowledgement is enough to correct the employee's behavior. This conversation should be documented in the employee's personnel file by placing a note outlining the date, time and conversation summary. This documentation is used only if the behavior is not corrected, and the supervisor must move on to the next step: a verbal warning.

VERBAL WARNING:

While both the awareness counseling and the verbal warning are "verbal", the verbal warning is a step further in the progressive discipline model. When meeting with an employee, the supervisor should remind the employee of the awareness counseling and tell them since the behavior has not corrected, the employee is now receiving a verbal warning. For example, if Bob comes in late the next morning, the supervisor should say, "Bob, yesterday I mentioned you came in late. You said everything was ok and it wouldn't happen again, but today you were late again. I am giving you a verbal warning because you were late today. I know you can turn this around, but if you don't, and you are late again, I will have to write you up. If there is anything you need from me, please let me know." A note about the verbal warning should go in the employee's personnel file, but the employee does not sign anything at this point.

WRITTEN WARNING:

If the employee's behavior continues, it is time to put the warning in writing. The written warning can be on a specific form used for employee discipline, or it can be a memo. The key is to document the employee's behavior that is not meeting expectations, provide examples of that behavior with dates and circumstances, provide what behavior is expected, and provide a place for the employee to write comments and sign the warning. If an employee refuses to sign the memo, that doesn't mean the warning doesn't exist.

Typically, I have a line that says, "I have read and received a copy of this memo" before the signature space. This line does not say anything about the employee agrees with the warning. If the employee refuses to sign the memo, tell the employee that does not negate the counseling session or the expectations outlined in the memo. Give the employee a copy of the memo and have the witness sign the memo stating the employee was given a copy of the memo but refused to sign it. (NOTE: It is always a good practice to have another manager or lead worker in the discipline meeting with you as a witness to what occurred in the meeting.) There is not a magic number of written warnings before an employee is terminated. It is dependent upon the actions of the employee.

NEXT STEPS:

What now? You've read the book and you feel more confident about managing employees but you want to learn more. Many people who have read this book have moved on to take my Home Study Course: **The Management Map: A 10-Week E-Course to Better Employee Management.** You can learn more at www. CourtSideHR.com.

If you have any questions, I'm happy to help. Email me at CBerg@ CourtSideHR.com.

LOOKING FOR A SPEAKER?

**If you enjoyed this book, Courtney Berg is the IDEAL profes-
sional speaker for your next event!**

Courtney Berg will leave your audiences laughing while they learn
the principles of management and human resources. Courtney's
high-energy presentations engage and entertain the audience AND
deliver a message that is dynamic and fun! Courtney believes we
can become great managers empowering our teams to accomplish
goals together. Through establishing expectations and constant
communication, managers will see their team's productivity in-
creases and more positive results are met.

If you would like to learn more about booking Courtney for a
keynote, breakout or workshop, please contact our office by calling 720-328-8870. You may also email your questions to: CBerg@
CourtSideHR.com.

SHARE THIS BOOK!

Quantity discounts are available. Call us for more information and
a quote. Personalized autographs copies are also available.

Made in the USA
San Bernardino, CA
12 August 2016